series

The Way of the Cross

Text
Sr. Karen Cavanagh, C.S.J.

Illustrations
Rita Goodwill

Cover Illustration
Michael Letwenko

THE REGINA PRESS
New York

THE WAY
OF THE CROSS

Since the time of Jesus, Christian people have always remembered the day on which Jesus died and the events of that Good Friday. In churches, chapels and some monastery gardens, people pray at carvings or pictures of the sad events of Jesus' passion and death.

We call this act of remembering "The Way of the Cross," and we call the events "Stations."

Most of Jesus' life was busy, happy and life giving. In the "Way of the Cross" we look at the one day in Jesus' life when He suffered and died.

Jesus suffered and died for love of God and love of us. His way of the cross was a way of love.

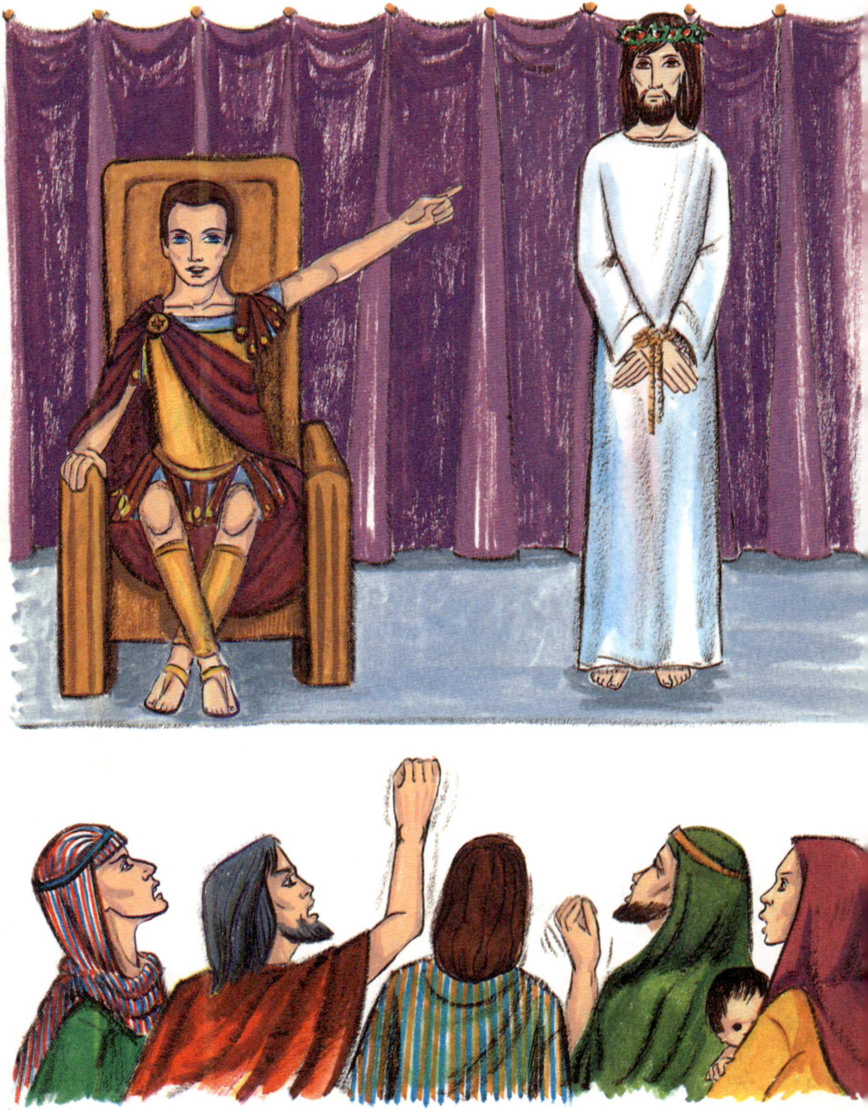

STATION ONE
JESUS MEETS PILATE

After Jesus was betrayed by His own apostle, Judas, He was taken to prison. Here they beat Him, made fun of Him and crowned Him with painful thorns.

Many of His enemies wanted Jesus out of the way—they wanted Him to die. They took Him to the palace of the governor, Pontius Pilate, who condemned Him to die on a cross.

Jesus, who was innocent, would die for love of God and love of us.

PRAYER: Dear Jesus, help me to keep on caring and loving even when others reject my love or wish me harm. Teach me forgiveness. Amen.

STATION TWO

JESUS CARRIES THE CROSS

The soldiers brought a large wooden cross to Jesus, and He took it upon His shoulders. It was rough and heavy. Jesus was weak, tired and hurting, but He began to carry the cross to Calvary, where He would die.

Sometimes the cross is called the "wood of salvation." On the day of His death, Jesus changed the cross into a sign of hope and salvation for each of us. The world's evil and hatred can be changed by God's love.

Jesus could change this cross, which He carried for love of God and love of us.

PRAYER: Dear Jesus, help me to carry my hurts and crosses. Give me Your love and teach me to talk with You. Amen.

STATION THREE
JESUS FALLS THE FIRST TIME

Jesus was so weak and tired as He walked the road to Calvary. Soon after He began to carry the cross, it became too heavy and too painful for His failing strength. Jesus fell to the ground under the weight of the cross. No one helped Him, and it seemed He would not be able to get up.

With courage and patience, He got up and began to walk the road again. He did this for love of God and love of us.

PRAYER: Dear Jesus, help me when my worries, fears or sadness weigh me down. Help me when I am too tired to begin again. Teach me Your courage and patience. Amen.

STATION FOUR
JESUS MEETS HIS MOTHER

Jesus' mother, Mary, was always a faithful follower of her son and His teachings. So many times she walked with Him as He told of God's love, cured the sick and helped those who were in pain. She loved Him and was so proud of Him.

On this walk to Calvary, Mary was still there with love for her son. Jesus was thankful that she was there for Him. The pain in their eyes spoke more than any words.

Without words Jesus knew that His mother loved Him. He had learned so much from Mary about the love of God and love of us.

PRAYER: Dear Jesus, please help me always to stand by the people I love and who love me. Help me to make my parents proud of me and teach me to love Your Mother, Mary. Amen.

SIMON HELPS JESUS CARRY THE CROSS

The cross seemed to get heavier with every step Jesus took. The soldiers noticed Jesus getting weaker. He was staggering and about to fall under the load on His shoulders.

The soldiers pulled a man from the crowd along the roadside. They forced him to help Jesus carry His cross. This stranger, whose name was Simon of Cyrene, was not one of Jesus' followers. Perhaps he was too frightened to refuse to help.

Simon did help Jesus to carry the cross. Sometimes we believe that his life was changed forever because he helped one who was weaker than he. This is what is meant by love of God and love of all others.

PRAYER: Dear Jesus, help me to see those who need my help. Help me to always lend a hand when asked or needed. Teach me to love all other people. Amen.

VERONICA WIPES THE FACE OF JESUS

Crowds had gathered all along the roadside of the way to Calvary—the way of the cross. Many of the people were there to see Jesus die. There were others, though, whose hearts broke as they saw Jesus' cruel suffering.

A woman named Veronica stepped out from the crowd into the roadway. As Jesus held His cross, Veronica held out a cloth—perhaps her own veil—and wiped the blood and sweat from the face of Jesus. Her simple kindness was one of the most loving things that happened to Jesus on that way. It helped Him to continue that day during which He showed His love of God and love of us.

PRAYER: Dear Jesus, help me to do the simplest acts of kindness for love of You. Teach me the power of a hug or a loving word of support. Amen.

JESUS FALLS A SECOND TIME

The walk to the Calvary hill was only half over and there still was a long distance to go. It seemed that again Jesus was made to carry His cross alone. It had become harder and harder for Him to stand up.

Jesus was out of breath and had no strength left. He stumbled, staggered and fell again.

The weight of the heavy cross almost crushed Him to the ground. How could this ever be the "wood of salvation"? Yet, Jesus again stood up, lifted His cross and began to walk forward. He was able to do this because of his strong love of God and love of us.

PRAYER: Dear Jesus, help me to know that You are always with me to lift me to Yourself and carry me through the difficult times. Teach me to give a hand to others who seem weighed down. Amen.

JESUS MEETS THE WOMEN AND CHILDREN

There were still others whose hearts broke when they saw Jesus in such pain. This group of women with their children were crying because so many had treated Jesus so cruelly.

Perhaps at that moment the women remembered how Jesus used to lift their children and hold them close to His heart. Now they wished they could hold the suffering Jesus in their arms.

Jesus told them to weep for themselves and for their children—for the cruelty of the world would touch them just as it had touched Him. His eyes were filled with His love of God and love of us.

PRAYER: Dear Jesus, help me to remember that I am Yours and that You hold me to Your heart at all times. Teach me to never be cruel or unloving. Amen.

JESUS FALLS A THIRD TIME

The crowds continued to watch Jesus struggle to carry the cross upon which He would die. Many mocked Him while others were filled with sadness. Jesus' followers were frightened. Some of them went into hiding.

Jesus came to the Calvary hill and tried to climb it. He had lost much strength; He was bleeding and so exhausted. Under the heavy weight of the cross, Jesus falls as if He was defeated.

Again He struggles to stand up. He will not be defeated because Jesus has chosen to live this way of the cross out of love of God and love of us.

PRAYER: Dear Jesus, help me to keep trying when I am feeling defeated. Help me to keep my eyes on You and teach me that You are my strength. Amen.

STATION TEN
JESUS IS STRIPPED OF HIS CLOTHES

Having been able to stand again and lift His cross Jesus took those final steps to the top of the Calvary hill. The soldiers who had guarded His way of the cross let Jesus drop the cross to the ground.

As Jesus stood in front of the crowds, He was again mocked and humiliated. The soldiers pulled off His clothes leaving Him embarrassed and without His dignity. He was treated as a common criminal. His enemies saw Him as a worthless human being.

His followers saw Him as the human being who lived the love of God and love of us.

PRAYER: Dear Jesus, help me to treat every person with dignity and respect. Help me to clothe them with love and teach me reverence for all life. Amen.

JESUS IS NAILED TO THE CROSS

In the time of Jesus, many criminals died on a cross. They were forced to die tied to a cross for all to see. Jesus was not tied. But His hands and feet were nailed to the wood before His cross was lifted for all to see. Everyone saw now that this "preacher" and "prophet" could not escape.

Jesus, who had released people from the prisons of blindness, sin, sickness and death, was now unable to get free. How could Jesus bear this pain and suffering? It could only be His great love of God and love of us.

PRAYER: Dear Jesus, help me always to be a person who frees and helps others who are trapped in pain and loneliness. Teach me to realize that You have won our freedom. Amen.

JESUS DIES UPON THE CROSS

Could this have been the "wood of salvation"? Could this cross be our hope and salvation?

Jesus called out to God, for He was frightened, feeling abandoned and about to die. He was full of pain. More important than His pain was His love of God and His care for His mother and for the people around Him. He asked them to care for one another.

With all His strength drained and His fear relieved, He gave His spirit over to God and died upon the cross. To the end, He spoke of His love of God and love of us.

PRAYER: Dear Jesus, help me to see death as another step in the life You give us. Teach me how to live and how to die. Amen.

JESUS IS PLACED IN MARY'S ARMS

When her child, Jesus, was still a baby, Mary was told that He would be rejected by many and that her heart would be broken.

When her child, Jesus, died on the cross, some friends gently took His body down from that cross and placed it in Mary's arms. Mary had held Jesus like this when He was a baby. Now His body had no life left in it.

Mary's heart broke with such sadness, emptiness and grief. She remembered her happy days with her son. She remembered her pride and she remembered the prophesy. Jesus had been rejected for His love of God and love of us.

PRAYER: Dear Jesus, help me to comfort those who lose someone they love. Teach me Your compassion. Amen.

JESUS IS LAID IN THE TOMB

When He was born in Bethlehem, the lively new baby Jesus rested in a borrowed manger. His mother cared for Him with love, joy and tenderness.

When He died on Calvary's hill, there was no place to rest His body. Friends placed His lifeless body in a borrowed tomb. This was the final stopping place of Jesus' way of the cross.

With love, broken hearts, and great tenderness, His mother and His friends cared for Him. They washed His body, anointed it with perfumes and covered it.

PRAYER: Dear Jesus, help me now to bring Your love of God and love of all people everywhere. Teach me to walk with You in life. Amen.

Jesus' way of the cross did not end in sadness but in joy. On Easter Sunday, He rose from the tomb gloriously alive.

For love of God and love of us, the cross became the "wood of salvation."